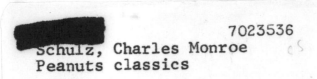

PEANUTS. CLASSICS

PEANUTS. CLASSICS

by Charles M. Schulz

HOLT, RINEHART AND WINSTON

New York • Chicago • San Francisco

Published simultaneously in Canada by Holt, Rinehart
and Winston of Canada, Limited

Library of Congress Catalog Number: 78-129092
Published, November, 1970
Second Printing, June, 1975
ISBN: 0-03-085078-9

Printed in the United States of America

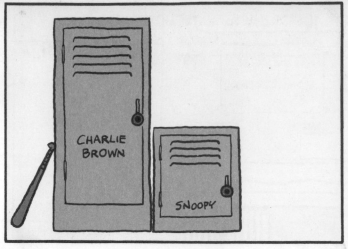

LET'S HUSTLE A LITTLE MORE ON THOSE FLY-BALLS!

C'MON! MOVE IN ON THOSE GROUNDERS! THROW THE BALL! DON'T HANG ON TO IT!

ALL RIGHT! EVERYBODY OVER HERE ON THE DOUBLE! LET'S GO!

OKAY, TEAM, THIS IS THE START OF A NEW SEASON, AND I HAVE A FEW WORDS TO SAY..

NOW, I THINK NO ONE WILL DENY THAT SPIRIT PLAYS AN IMPORTANT ROLE IN WINNING BALL GAMES..

SOME MIGHT SAY THAT IT PLAYS THE MOST IMPORTANT ROLE..

THE DESIRE TO WIN IS WHAT MAKES A TEAM GREAT..WINNING IS EVERYTHING!

THE ONLY THING THAT MATTERS IS TO COME IN FIRST PLACE!

WHAT I'M TRYING TO SAY IS THAT NO ONE EVER REMEMBERS WHO COMES IN SECOND PLACE!

I DO, CHARLIE BROWN... IN 1928, THE GIANTS AND PHILADELPHIA FINISHED SECOND.. IN 1929, IT WAS PITTSBURGH AND THE YANKEES.. IN 1930, IT WAS CHICAGO AND WASHINGTON.. IN 1931, IT WAS THE GIANTS AND THE YANKEES.. IN 1932, IT WAS PITTSBURGH AND...

AND ANOTHER GREAT SEASON GETS UNDERWAY!

EVERYBODY OUT TO THE MOUND!

ALL RIGHT, TEAM...THIS IS OUR FIRST GAME OF THE SEASON..

IF WE ALL SHOW THE RIGHT SPIRIT, I THINK WE CAN WIN THIS ONE

LET'S TRY TO ENCOURAGE EACH OTHER...LET'S HEAR A LITTLE CHATTER OUT THERE, OKAY?

YOU'RE BEAUTIFUL, KID!

YEARS FROM NOW WHEN I GET DRAFTED, THE ARMY EXAMINER WILL ASK ME WHY I HAVE THIS KITE WITH ME, AND I'LL SAY, "DON'T ASK SUCH STUPID QUESTIONS"

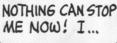

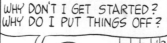

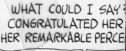

MY REPORT IS ON AFRICA

ACTUALLY, WHAT I MEAN TO SAY IS THAT MY REPORT WOULD HAVE BEEN ON AFRICA IF.... WELL, MY INTENTIONS WERE.....

IT SEEMS THAT I JUST NEVER QUITE GOT AROUND TO...WELL, YOU KNOW HOW IT GOES SOMETIMES, AND I JUST...I JUST NEVER..

I THROW MYSELF UPON THE MERCY OF THE COURT!

THERE'S A GREAT BIG PURPLE AND GREEN AND YELLOW SPIDER WITH FORTY THOUSAND LEGS CRAWLING UP YOUR BACK!

NOBODY EVER BELIEVES MY APRIL FOOL JOKES

SO YOU'RE GETTING A LITTLE WET..

DON'T LOOK SO DEPRESSED...

REMEMBER, IT RAINS ON THE JUST AND THE UNJUST

BUT WHY US IN-BETWEENS?

THE GRASS IS SOFT
IT'S COOL!

I FEEL FREE!!

RUNNING AROUND IN THE GRASS IN YOUR BARE FEET CAN BE VERY EXCITING...

AFTER A FEW YEARS, HOWEVER, THE EXCITEMENT WEARS OFF!

HERE'S THE WORLD FAMOUS GOLF PRO TEEING OFF ON THE FIRST HOLE AT THE MASTERS...

AS HE WALKS DOWN THE FIRST FAIRWAY, HE IS FOLLOWED BY THAT HUGE THRONG OF HIS ADMIRERS KNOWN AS "SNOOPY'S SQUAD"

WINTER RULES?

HERE WE GO... THE FIRST PITCH OF THE SEASON..

POW!

IT'S KIND OF PEACEFUL LYING HERE AMONG THE DANDELIONS..

WHAT IN THE WORLD ARE ALL THESE DANDELIONS DOING ON THE PITCHER'S MOUND?

THEY **GREW** THERE! AND MY STUPID GIRL-OUTFIELDERS WON'T LET ME CUT THEM DOWN! THEY SAY THEY'RE **PRETTY**, AND I LOOK **CUTE** STANDING HERE AMONG THEM!

THEY'RE RIGHT...YOU **DO** LOOK KIND OF CUTE STANDING THERE..

HOLD YOUR CHIN UP, CHARLIE BROWN..

I'M GOING TO TICKLE YOU WITH THIS DANDELION..IF YOUR CHIN TURNS YELLOW, IT MEANS YOU LIKE BUTTER..

4-6

HEY, LOOK! CHARLIE BROWN LIKES BUTTER!

I WONDER IF MY FONDNESS FOR DAIRY PRODUCTS WILL HELP US WIN BALL GAMES

WHY, CHARLIE BROWN! YOU CUT DOWN ALL THE DANDELIONS!

YES, I CUT DOWN ALL THE DANDELIONS! THIS IS A PITCHER'S MOUND, NOT A FLOWER GARDEN!

SPEAKING OF FLOWER GARDENS, I'LL BET A CIRCLE OF DAFFODILS WOULD LOOK NICE AROUND THIS MOUND, DON'T YOU THINK SO?

OH, YES, VERY NICE...OR EVEN SOME MARIGOLDS..

I CAN'T STAND IT!

WELL, WE LOST THE FIRST GAME OF THE SEASON AGAIN!

I SHOULDN'T LET IT BOTHER ME, BUT IT DOES...

WE ALWAYS SEEM TO LOSE THE FIRST GAME OF THE SEASON AND THE LAST GAME OF THE SEASON..

AND ALL THE STUPID GAMES IN-BETWEEN!

I THINK SOMETHING'S WRONG WITH MY TONGUE..

WHEN I TRY TO SAY, "BLAHLALAALAA," IT SAYS, "BRZAARZAZAA" INSTEAD...

DO YOU THINK SOMETHING COULD BE WRONG WITH MY TONGUE?

I THINK SOMETHING'S WRONG WITH YOUR WHOLE HEAD!

DEAR LITTLE RED-HAIRED GIRL, I HAVE BEEN WANTING TO MEET YOU FOR A LONG TIME.

I THINK YOU ARE WONDERFUL. WOULD YOU CARE IF I CAME OVER TO YOUR HOUSE TO SEE YOU? WE COULD SIT ON YOUR FRONT STEPS AND TALK.

I MUST HAVE A FEVER!

IF I WERE YOU, CHARLIE BROWN, I'D FORGET THAT LITTLE RED-HAIRED GIRL..YOU'RE NOT HER KIND..

WHO'S KIND AM I?

NOW, THAT'S A GOOD QUESTION! YES, SIR, THAT'S A VERY GOOD QUESTION!

BOY, YOU'VE SURE GOT ME THERE.. WHO'S KIND ARE YOU? WOW! THAT'S A REAL STICKLER!

THAT'S A PUZZLER IF I EVER HEARD ONE! YES, SIR! THAT'S A ROUGH ONE! THAT'S A POSER! THAT'S A..

OH, GOOD GRIEF!

THERE'S THE HOUSE WHERE THAT LITTLE RED-HAIRED GIRL LIVES...

I WISH I HAD TWO PONIES... I'D RIDE UP TO HER FRONT DOOR, AND SAY, "HI! WOULD YOU LIKE TO GO FOR A RIDE? YOU MAY HAVE THE SPOTTED PONY!" AND WE'D RIDE OFF.

THEN, WHEN WE'D GET WAY OUT IN THE COUNTRY, I'D HELP HER DOWN OFF THE PONY, AND HOLD HER HAND, AND WE'D SIT UNDER A TREE WHILE THE PONIES GRAZED... SIGH...

WHY AREN'T YOU TWO PONIES?

I KNEW WE'D GET AROUND TO THAT!

IT'S BEEN A LONG TIME SINCE YOU SAID YOU LIKED ME

I'VE **NEVER** SAID I LIKED YOU!

I THINK I'LL GO HOME AND SLAM ALL THE DOORS

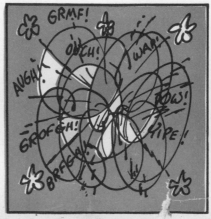

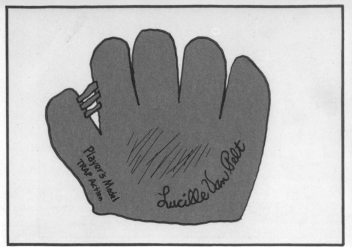

WHAT IN THE WORLD ARE YOU DOING?

ONE MINUTE YOU'RE IN CENTER FIELD, AND THE NEXT MINUTE YOU'RE GONE! WHAT KIND OF BALL PLAYER ARE YOU?!!

I WAS STANDING OUT THERE IN CENTER FIELD, CHARLIE BROWN, AND I WAS PAYING ATTENTION LIKE YOU ALWAYS TELL ME TO DO..

SUDDENLY, OUT OF NOWHERE, I HEARD A PIECE OF CAKE CALLING ME!

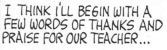

HOW'S IT GOING?

PRETTY WELL, I THINK...IT'S NOT EASY TO PAINT WHILE YOU'RE LYING ON YOUR BACK..

PUTTING UP THE SCAFFOLDING WAS THE HARDEST JOB

IT'S GOING TO BE NICE HAVING A MURAL ON THE CEILING.

I HEAR LINUS IS PAINTING A MURAL ON THE CEILING OF SNOOPY'S DOGHOUSE

YES, WOULD YOU LIKE TO GO IN, AND SEE IT?

LINUS, I'M BRINGING FRIEDA IN TO SEE THE MURAL...EXPLAIN WHAT YOU'RE DOING, WILL YOU?

WELL, I'M TRYING TO TELL THE STORY OF CIVILIZATION...THIS WHOLE SECTION OVER HERE WILL BE DEVOTED TO THE EGYPTIANS...

IT STAGGERS THE IMAGINATION!

THE STORY OF CIVILIZATION PAINTED ON THE CEILING OF A DOGHOUSE! LINUS, YOU'RE FANTASTIC!

THANK YOU, CHARLIE BROWN

RIGHT NOW I'M WORKING ON THE STRUGGLES OF THE MACCABEES WHICH BEGAN AROUND 167 B.C.

I HAD A LITTLE TROUBLE WITH ANTIOCHUS EPIPHANES BECAUSE I DIDN'T KNOW WHAT HE LOOKED LIKE

A LACK OF KNOWLEDGE FORGIVABLE IN A MURAL PAINTER WHO IS ONLY SIX YEARS OLD!

SNOOPY, YOU SHOULD SEE THIS MURAL!

LINUS HAS PAINTED THE ENTIRE STORY OF CIVILIZATION ON THE CEILING OF YOUR DOGHOUSE...

YOU SHOULD BE VERY IMPRESSED

I AM...THINK WHAT IT DO FOR THE RESALE VALUE

WHAT?

YOU'RE NOT EVEN GOING TO LOOK AT IT?!!

LINUS PAINTS A MURAL OF THE ENTIRE STORY OF CIVILIZATION ON THE CEILING OF HIS DOGHOUSE, AND HE'S NOT EVEN GOING TO LOOK AT IT!

FOR MY KIND, THE STORY C CIVILIZATION HAS ALWAYS LEF MUCH TO BE DESIRED!

 TEN BILLION AND ONE, TEN BILLION AND TWO,

 TEN BILLION AND THREE, TEN BILLION AND FOUR,

 AND ALSO WHEN I TALK TO PEOPLE, I FIND THAT THEY DON'T REALLY LISTEN TO ME..

 I FIND THAT I CAN'T SEEM TO HOLD A PERSON'S ATTENTION... WHEN I TALK TO PEOPLE, THEIR MINDS SORT OF WANDER OFF, AND THEY STARE INTO SPACE, AND...

 ...AND...AND....

 SOMETIMES I LIE AWAKE AT NIGHT AND THINK ABOUT THAT LITTLE RED-HAIRED GIRL...

 I DON'T EVER WANT TO FORGET HER FACE, BUT IF I DON'T FORGET HER FACE, I'LL GO CRAZY...

 HOW CAN I REMEMBER THE FACE I CAN'T FORGET?

 SUDDENLY I'M WRITING COUNTRY WESTERN MUSIC!

 LAST NIGHT I DREAMED ABOUT THAT LITTLE RED-HAIRED GIRL..

 IT WAS ALL VERY DEPRESSING.. I WISH I WOULDN'T HAVE THOSE DREAMS...

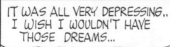 IT'S TOO BAD WE CAN'T KNOW AHEAD OF TIME WHAT WE'RE GOING TO DREAM

 MAYBE THEY COULD PUBLISH REVIEWS

 PSST...HEY, FRANKLIN, IS THE THIRD QUESTION "TRUE" OR "FALSE"?

 I DON'T KNOW..

 WHY DON'T YOU PUT DOWN TRUE AND I'LL PUT DOWN FALSE? THAT WAY ONE OF US WILL BE RIGHT.. ONE OF US WILL ALSO BE WRONG...

 LEARNING IS AN EXCITING ADVENTURE!

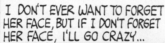

WILL YOU HELP ME WITH MY "TIMES TABLES," DEAR BROTHER?

OKAY, LET'S RUN THROUGH THE TWO'S FIRST...

WHAT IS TWO TIMES SEVEN? ONE MILLION?

YOU'RE GUESSING!

YOU REALLY NEED WORK ON YOUR TIMES-TABLES, SALLY, I CAN SEE THAT...

LET'S TRY THE THREES... HOW MUCH IS THREE TIMES ZERO?

FOUR THOUSAND? SIX? ELEVENTY TWELVE? FIFTY-QUILLION? OVERLY-EIGHT? TWIDDELY-TWO?

WELL? AM I GETTING CLOSER? ACTUALLY, IT'S KIND OF HARD TO SAY!

MY MOTHER IS WATCHING ME OUT OF THE WINDOW..

MOTHERS FEEL SECURE WHEN THEY SEE A CHILD OF THEIRS PLAYING IN A SANDBOX...

✳ SIGH ✳

SHE'S SECURE, AND I'M BORED TO DEATH!

I DON'T WORRY ABOUT THE WORLD COMING TO AN END ANY MORE..

THE WAY I FIGURE IT, THE WORLD CAN'T COME TO AN END TODAY BECAUSE IT IS ALREADY TOMORROW IN SOME OTHER PART OF THE WORLD!

ISN'T THAT A COMFORTING THEORY?

I'VE NEVER FELT SO COMFORTED IN ALL MY LIFE

FELICITAS EST PARVUS CANIS CALIDUS

THAT'S LATIN FOR "HAPPINESS IS A WARM PUPPY"

I CAN'T STAND IT!

THINK ABOUT THIS DAY FOR A MOMENT, CHARLIE BROWN..

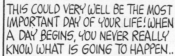
THIS COULD VERY WELL BE THE MOST IMPORTANT DAY OF YOUR LIFE! WHEN A DAY BEGINS, YOU NEVER REALLY KNOW WHAT IS GOING TO HAPPEN..

YOU'RE RIGHT, LUCY, AND THIS VERY 'ORDINARY DAY' COULD TURN OUT TO BE THE MOST IMPORTANT DAY OF MY LIFE!

BUT IT PROBABLY WON'T!

BUT FIFTY IS MORE THAN TWENTY-FIVE!

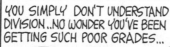
YOU SIMPLY DON'T UNDERSTAND DIVISION..NO WONDER YOU'VE BEEN GETTING SUCH POOR GRADES...

YOU CAN'T MAKE FIFTY GO INTO TWENTY-FIVE!

YOU CAN IF YOU PUSH IT!

YOU LOOK KIND OF DEPRESSED, CHARLIE BROWN

I WORRY ABOUT SCHOOL A LOT...

I ALSO WORRY ABOUT MY WORRYING SO MUCH ABOUT SCHOOL..

MY ANXIETIES HAVE ANXIETIES

OKAY, GANG, LET'S TALK IT UP OUT THERE!

C'MON, LET'S GET THIS GUY OUT HE CAN'T HIT IT HE CAN'T EVEN SEE IT HE'S NO GOOD C'MON LET'S THROW IT RIGHT ON PAST HIM GIVE 'IM THE OL' BEAN BALL LET'S PITCH IT RIGHT ON PAST 'IM, BOY

C'MON HE'S NO HITTER HE HITS LIKE MY GRANDMOTHER THROW IT TO 'IM DON'T BE AFRAID OF THIS GUY HE'S NO HITTER NO HITTER AT ALL NO HITTER UP THERE LET'S JUST THROW RIGHT PAST 'IM HE'LL NEVER HIT IT NOBODY TO WORRY ABOUT THROW IT TO 'IM BOY

MAYBE I SHOULDN'T HAVE SAID ANYTHING..

WHAT'S THE MATTER WITH ALL YOU GUYS, ARE YOU ASLEEP OR SOMETHING?

LET'S TALK IT UP! LET'S HEAR SOME CHATTER OUT THERE!

I COULD WHINE A LITTLE..

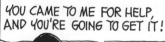

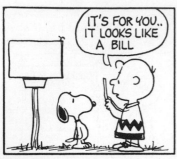

Panel 1: VERY INTERESTING

WHAT'S VERY INTERESTING?

Panel 2: LISTEN... THESE ARE WORDS TO PARENTS FROM DR. HORWICH...

Panel 3: "IF HOMEWORK IS TO BE BENEFICIAL TO A CHILD, IT SHOULD NOT CONSIST OF ASSIGNMENTS IMPOSED AS A PUNISHMENT FOR BEHAVIOR TOTALLY UNRELATED TO THE WORK ASSIGNED.."

Panel 4: THAT'S GOOD THINKING! DR. HORWICH, YOU'RE A GEM!

Panel 5: "THE CHILD WHO IS TARDY IN ARRIVING AT SCHOOL, SHOULD NOT HAVE TO READ AN EXTRA TWENTY PAGES AT HOME AS PUNISHMENT FOR SUCH BEHAVIOR.."

THAT'S WHAT I SAY!

Panel 6: "CHILDREN IN ELEMENTARY SCHOOLS SHOULD NOT BE GIVEN ASSIGNMENTS ALL OF WHICH COMBINED WILL TAKE LONGER THAN ONE HOUR TO COMPLETE"

HEAR! HEAR!

Panel 7: "THE CHILD SHOULD NOT BE ASKED TO SPEND THE ENTIRE TIME BETWEEN DINNER AND BEDTIME DOING HOMEWORK.."

AMEN! HOW RIGHT CAN YOU GET?

Panel 8: "WHENEVER THERE IS HOMEWORK, THERE MUST BE A THREE-MEMBER TEAM..THE TEACHER, THE CHILD AND THE PARENT.."

I FULLY AGREE

Panel 9: LET THE PRINCIPAL KEEP OUT OF IT!

Panel 10: IT'S NOT OFTEN THAT A PERSON GETS THE CHANCE TO READ TO SOMEONE WHO SHOWS SUCH ENTHUSIASM!

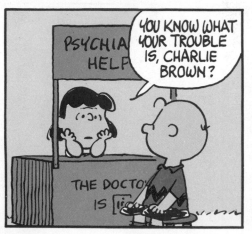

HAPPY FATHER'S DAY from your rare gem.

HI, ROY...I SUPPOSE YOU'RE WONDERING WHAT I'M DOING...

I'VE JUST MADE MY DAD A HAND-MADE FATHER'S DAY CARD..

EVERY NOW AND THEN MY DAD SAYS TO ME, "PEPPERMINT PATTY, DO YOU KNOW WHAT YOU ARE?" AND I ALWAYS SAY, "NO"....THEN HE SAYS TO ME, "YOU ARE A RARE GEM!" AND WE BOTH LAUGH...

SO YOU SEE, I'VE MADE A CARD FOR HIM ... "HAPPY FATHER'S DAY FROM YOUR RARE GEM"

THAT'S VERY NICE..

THANK YOU..I'LL PUT IT ON TOP OF HIS DRESSER WHERE HE'LL SEE IT...

ACTUALLY, ANYONE WHO GIVES HIS DAD A FATHER'S DAY CARD IS A RARE GEM...

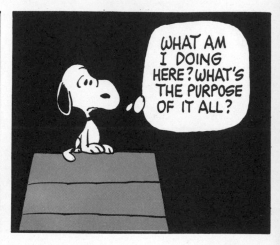

WAAH!

WHAT'S THE MATTER, SALLY? WHAT HAPPENED? WHY ARE YOU CRYING?

I DON'T KNOW...

I WAS JUMPING ROPE.... EVERYTHING WAS ALL RIGHT... WHEN... I DON'T KNOW...

SUDDENLY IT ALL SEEMED SO FUTILE !

SCHROEDER, WHAT WOULD HAPPEN IF YOU AND I GOT MARRIED SOMEDAY, AND I GOT TIRED OF FIXING YOUR BREAKFAST?

I MEAN, WHAT WOULD HAPPEN IF I DECIDED I'D RATHER SLEEP IN THE MORNING?

I CAN'T STAND IT...

SAY, FOR INSTANCE, I GOT TIRED OF GETTING UP EVERY MORNING TO FIX YOUR BREAKFAST, AND JUST SUDDENLY DECIDED I'D RATHER SLEEP LATE EVERY MORNING...

I MEAN, WHAT WOULD YOUR REACTION BE?

ROWRR!!

WELL, PERHAPS I COULD SLEEP LATE ON WEEKENDS...

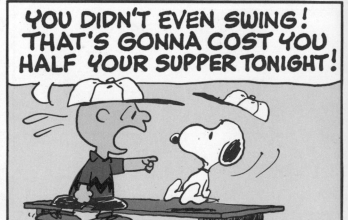

BONK!

I CAN'T STAND IT!

OKAY, LUCY, WHERE WERE YOU ON THAT FLY BALL? LET'S START PAYING ATTENTION!

BLEAH!

AND HOW ABOUT YOU? YOU WERE OUT OF POSITION ON THAT DOUBLE-PLAY BALL! YOU BETTER LOOK ALIVE!

BLEAH!

AND YOU SURE HAVEN'T BEEN DOING MUCH OF A JOB BEHIND THE PLATE, SCHROEDER! HOW ABOUT SHOWING SOME LIFE BACK THERE, HUH? HOW ABOUT IT?

BLEAH!

MAYBE I WAS TOO HARD ON THEM...AFTER ALL, I HAVEN'T BEEN DOING TOO WELL MYSELF...IN FACT, MY PITCHING HAS BEEN LOUSY!

BY GOLLY, CHARLIE BROWN, YOU'D BETTER START PITCHING BETTER BALL!! YOU'D BETTER BUCKLE DOWN OUT HERE!

BLEAH!

SCHULZ

STOP LOOKING SO BORED ALL THE TIME!

LIFE ISN'T THAT BAD...THE LEAST YOU CAN DO IS **LOOK** INTERESTED!

LOOKING BORED IS EASIER ON THE EYES..

MY MOM AND DAD WERE GOING ON A LITTLE VACATION, BUT THEY CHANGED THEIR MINDS

MOM IS KIND OF A WORRIER

SHE SAYS, WHAT IF THEY WERE DRIVING ALONG THE FREEWAY DOING ABOUT SEVENTY, AND SUDDENLY SOMETHING WENT WRONG WITH THE GLOVE COMPARTMENT?

THAT **IS** SOMETHING TO WORRY ABOUT

YOU DON'T CONFORM AT ALL TO MY IDEA OF WHAT A LITTLE BROTHER SHOULD BE!

I SHALL IMMEDIATELY BEGIN A COURSE OF SELF-EXAMINATION TO FIND OUT WHERE MY FAULTS LIE SO THAT I MAY RESEMBLE MORE CLOSELY THE IMAGE YOU WISH ME TO ATTAIN!

LITTLE BROTHERS ARE BORN WIT A SARCASM THAT IS HANDED DO FROM GENERATION TO GENERATIC

I SHOULD HAVE COME TO SEE YOU EARLIER THIS MORNING, BUT..

PSYCHIATRI HELP 5¢

THE DOCTOR IS IN

BUT YOU HAVE IATROPHOBIA, DON'T YOU? THAT'S A FEAR OF GOING TO THE DOCTOR! I'LL BET YOU HAVE IATROPHOBIA!

WHAT A TERRIBLE THING! YOU COULD HAVE BEEN HERE BEING CURED OF ALL YOUR PROBLEMS, BUT YOUR IATROPHOBIA KEPT YOU AWAY! WHAT A TERRIBLE THING!

ACTUALLY, MY MOTHER WANT ME TO STAY HOME, AND CLEAN UP MY ROOM!

THE DOCTOR IS IN

I THINK I'VE MADE A NEW THEOLOGICAL DISCOVERY...

WHAT IS IT?

IF YOU HOLD YOUR HANDS UPSIDE DOWN, YOU GET TH OPPOSITE OF WHAT YOU PRAY F

I'VE BEEN THINKING ABOUT SOMETHING...

IN THE BIG LEAGUES, WHEN A TEAM GETS A RALLY STARTED, SOMEONE BLOWS A TRUMPET AND EVERYONE YELLS, "CHARGE!!"

DO YOU THINK WE COULD DO THAT, CHARLIE BROWN?

I DON'T KNOW...WE'VE NEVER HAD A RALLY...

LITTLE GIRLS NEED BIG BROTHERS..

BIG BROTHERS ARE STRONG, AND WHEN YOU'RE WALKING ALONG THE STREET THEY MAKE YOU FEEL SECURE

SORT OF!

A FINE BIG BROTHER YOU ARE!

THAT BULLY OVER AT THE PLAYGROUND PUSHED ME DOWN, AND YOU DIDN'T EVEN HELP ME!

EVEN IF YOU **KNEW** HE COULD BEAT YOU UP, YOU SHOULD HAVE RUSHED IN TO HELP ME!

I THINK I WOULD HAVE MADE A BETTER YOUNGER BROTHER

I'VE LOST THE RESPECT OF MY LITTLE SISTER..

YESTERDAY A BULLY PUSHED HER DOWN OVER AT THE PLAYGROUND, AND I JUST STOOD THERE...I WAS SO AFRAID I DIDN'T EVEN HELP HER. NOW, I'VE LOST HER RESPECT...

I KNOW HOW YOU MUST FEEL, CHARLIE BROWN...**DON'T** YOU WISH YOU HAD IT ALL TO DO OVER?

NO, I'D PROBABLY DO THE SAME THING!

LUCY'S GOING WITH ME OVER TO THE PLAYGROUND

IF **YOU** CAN'T PROTECT ME FROM BULLIES, **SHE** CAN!!

I'VE BEEN TAKEN OUT FOR A PINCH-HITTER!

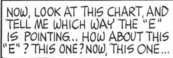

I HATE THESE PAR FIVES THAT YOU CAN'T REACH IN FORTY-TWO...

YOU DON'T THINK MY BROTHER AND I GET ALONG VERY WELL, DO YOU?

YOU JUST WAIT....SOMEDAY, AFTER WE'RE GROWN, WE'LL BE VERY CLOSE!

WHAT DOES SHE MEAN BY "CLOSE"?

WE MAY BOTH LIVE ON THE SAME CONTINENT!

I THINK I HAVE A VERY CUTE SMILE

I'VE NEVER HEARD YOU SAY I HAVE A CUTE SMILE, SCHROEDER...DO YOU THINK I HAVE A CUTE SMILE?

OH, YES, I THINK YOU HAVE THE CUTEST SMILE OF ANYONE SINCE THE WORLD BEGAN..

EVEN WHEN HE SAYS IT HE DOESN'T SAY IT!

I NEED YOUR OPINION, LINUS...

I'M GOING TO SMILE NOW AND I WANT YOU TO TELL ME IF I HAVE A CUTE SMILE......

SURE, YOUR SMILE IS KIND OF CUTE ALTHOUGH IT LOOKS SORT OF LIKE AN UPSIDE-DOWN CROQUET WICKET..

WE HAVEN'T PLAYED CROQUET A LONG TIME..I'VE ALWAYS KIND OF LIKED CROQUET..

SIGH

DO YOU THINK I HAVE A CUTE SMILE, CHARLIE BROWN?

OH, YES...I THINK IT'S VERY FUNNY..

WAP!

I'VE ALWAYS BEEN A GOOD SPELLER, BUT I'VE NEVER BEEN VERY GOOD WITH DEFINITIONS..

ALL RIGHT, SNOOPY, THIS IS THE LAST OF THE NINTH...WE NEED ONE RUN TO TIE UP THE GAME..

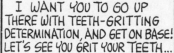

I WANT YOU TO GO UP THERE WITH TEETH-GRITTING DETERMINATION, AND GET ON BASE! LET'S SEE YOU GRIT YOUR TEETH...

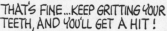

THAT'S FINE...KEEP GRITTING YOUR TEETH, AND YOU'LL GET A HIT!

I FEEL LIKE A FOOL...

LOOK AT THAT! SNOOPY GOT A HIT! WE'RE STILL IN THE GAME!

IT'S THAT TEETH-GRITTING DETERMINATION THAT DOES IT! NOW, LINUS, YOU GET UP THERE, AND GET A HIT, TOO...LET'S SEE YOU GRIT YOUR TEETH...

GREAT! IF YOU GRIT YOUR TEETH, YOU CAN'T FAIL!

IF I GET HIT IN THE MOUTH, I CAN SURE FAIL

LOOK AT THAT! LINUS GOT A HIT, TOO! I KNEW WE STILL HAD A CHANCE!

IF YOU GRIT YOUR TEETH, AND SHOW REAL DETERMINATION, YOU ALWAYS HAVE A CHANCE! YOU'RE UP NEXT, LUCY...LET'S SEE YOU GRIT YOUR TEETH...

FANTASTIC! YOU'LL SCARE THEIR PITCHER TO DEATH! KEEP GRITTING YOUR TEETH, AND GO GET A HIT!

GET A HIT?! I CAN'T EVEN SEE WHERE I'M GOIN'

LUCY GRITTED HER TEETH, AND GOT AN INFIELD SINGLE! THE BASES ARE LOADED!

IT JUST SHOWS WHAT TEETH-GRITTING DETERMINATION CAN DO! WHO'S OUR NEXT TEETH-GRITTING HERO?

WHO'S UP NEXT? WHO'S UP NEXT?

YOU ARE!

GRIT YOUR TEETH, CHARLIE BROWN

WHY DO I ALWAYS HAVE TO BE UP WHEN THE BASES ARE LOADED?

JUST DO WHAT YOU TOLD ALL THE OTHERS.... GRIT YOUR TEETH, AND GET A HIT!

COME ON, CHARLIE BROWN... LET'S SEE YOU GRIT YOUR TEETH...THAT'S THE WAY..

GOOD GRIEF!

CLICKETY CLICK CLICK CHATTER CHATTER

CLICKET CLICK CLICK CLICK CHATTER

SCHULZ

OH, NO! MY FAVORITE PLAYER, JOE SHLABOTNIK, HAS BEEN SENT DOWN TO THE MINORS AGAIN!

HE'S GOING TO PLAY FOR STUMPTOWN IN THE GREEN GRASS LEAGUE...

I HOPE THE FANS IN STUMPTOWN APPRECIATE WHAT A GREAT PLAYER THEY'RE GETTING

I BET HE'LL LEAD STUMPTOWN TO ITS FIRST PENNANT!

WITH A .004 BATTING AVERAGE?

DEAR JOE SHLABOTNIK,
I WAS SORRY TO HEAR OF YOUR BEING SENT TO STUMPTOWN IN THE GREEN GRASS LEAGUE.

I THINK IT WAS UNFAIR OF THEM TO SEND YOU TO THE MINORS JUST BECAUSE YOU ONLY GOT ONE HIT IN TWO HUNDRED AND FORTY TIMES AT BAT.

DON'T BE DISCOURAGED. LOTS OF GOOD PLAYERS GET OFF TO A SLOW START.
YOUR FAN,
Charlie Brown

P.S. I SAW YOU ON TV THE DAY YOU GOT YOUR HIT.

DID YOU SEE HOW I STRUCK OUT THAT LAST KID? PRETTY GOOD PITCHING, HUH?

YEAH, THAT WAS THAT KID WHO'S BEEN SICK IN BED ALL WINTER...HIS DOCTOR SAYS HE'S GOING TO BE ALL RIGHT, BUT TO GET OUT IN THE SUN...

HE ALSO DOESN'T SEE VERY WELL, AND HE'S NEVER PLAYED BASEBALL BEFORE...

SOMETIMES A CATCHER CAN KNOW TOO MUCH ABOUT THE OPPOSITION...

AAUGH! A SPIDER!!

THERE'S A SPIDER ON THE BALL! WE CAN'T PICK UP THE BALL, CHARLIE BROWN! THERE'S A SPIDER ON IT!

IT WILL BE INTERESTING TO SEE IF THE OFFICIAL SCORER GIVES THE HITTER CREDIT FOR A HOME RUN..

WE'RE SURE BUILDING UP A BIG LEAD IN THIS GAME, CHARLIE BROWN..

I'LL SAY WE ARE! WE'VE GOT THIS GAME COLD..WE CAN'T LOSE!

THE ONLY THING THAT COULD KEEP US FROM WINNING TODAY WOULD BE TO HAVE THE GAME RAINED OUT!

I CAN'T STAND IT!

DEAR MOM AND DAD, THINGS ARE GOING BETTER HERE AT CAMP.

Yesterday I met this kid named Charlie Brown.

HE WAS VERY LONESOME, BUT I THINK I HAVE HELPED HIM.

He's the kind who makes a good temporary friend.

STRIKE THREE!

WHAT'S THE MATTER, KID? AIN'TCHA NEVER PLAYED BASEBALL BEFORE?!!

WHY DIDN'T YOU TELL HIM, CHARLIE BROWN? WHY DIDN'T YOU TELL HIM ABOUT HOW YOU'RE THE MANAGER OF A TEAM AT HOME?

SOMEHOW, MENTIONING A TEAM THAT HAS THREE GIRL-OUTFIELDERS AND A DOG-SHORTSTOP DIDN'T SEEM QUITE APPROPRIATE!

WELL, SO LONG, CHARLIE BROWN... IT'S BEEN NICE KNOWING YOU..

IT'S BEEN NICE KNOWING YOU, TOO, ROY....HAVE A GOOD TRIP HOME..

FOR THE FIRST TIME IN MY LIFE I FEEL I REALLY HELPED SOMEONE...HE WAS LONESOME, AND I BECAME HIS FRIEND...

WHAT AN ACCOMPLISHMENT!

WELL, HERE I AM ON THE BUS RETURNING HOME FROM CAMP

HERE'S THE STATION..I'M ALMOST HOME...I CAN'T BELIEVE IT...

LOOK! THERE'S SOME KIDS ALL LINED UP JUST GETTING READY TO LEAVE FOR CAMP...

LET 'EM GO! I'VE DONE MY HITCH!!

OH, BOY! IS IT EVER GOOD TO BE BACK HOME!

HI, LUCY! I'M BACK!
YOU'RE WHAT?

I SAID, I'M BACK!

HAVE YOU BEEN AWAY?

HERE'S THE SECRET AGENT CARRYING OUT HIS DANGEROUS MISSION...

HE HAS BEEN ASSIGNED TO GET INFORMATION ABOUT THE DISAPPEARANCE OF A VALUABLE BLANKET

AH! THERE IS THE ENEMY AGENT WHO KNOWS THE SECRET! I WILL WIN MY WAY INTO HER CONFIDENCE WITH A ROMANTIC OVERTURE...

WHAT IN THE WORLD ?!?

HELLO? OH, HI, GRAMMA, HOW ARE YOU? ME? OH, I'M FINE, I GUESS...

HOW ARE YOU AND YOUR SMOKING? YOU HAVE? WELL, THAT'S GREAT... NO, I HAVEN'T TOUCHED MY BLANKET FOR TWO WEEKS...

I DON'T EVEN KNOW WHERE IT IS... LUCY HID IT.....NO, SHE WON'T TELL...NO...

I THINK IT WOULD TAKE A SECRET AGENT TO GET HER TO TELL WHERE IT IS...

GET AWAY FROM ME, YOU STUPID DOG!

MMM! SMAK SMAK SMAK SMAK!!

WELL, IT'S TIME FOR THE BLANKET BURNING...

THE WHAT ?!

YOU'VE GONE WITHOUT YOUR BLANKET FOR TWO WEEKS NOW.. THAT PROVES YOU NO LONGER REALLY NEED IT!

WE WILL NOW HOLD A "BLANKET BURNING" WHICH WILL SYMBOLIZE YOUR NEW PSYCHOLOGICAL FREEDOM!

COULDN'T WE MAYBE USE A SYMBOLIC BLANKET ??

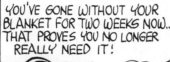

THE "BLANKET BURNING" HAS BEGUN!

AS I TOSS YOUR BLANKET INTO THE TRASH BURNER, YOUR INSECURITIES ARE SYMBOLICALLY DESTROYED FOREVER!!

THERE! YOU ARE NOW FREE FROM THE TERRIBLE HOLD IT ONCE HAD ON YOU... YOU ARE A NEW PERSON!

AAUGHH!!

GIVE ME BACK THAT BLANKET!

NO ONE IS GOING TO CURE ME OF ANYTHING! WHO ARE YOU TO TELL ME WHAT TO DO? WHO IS GRAMMA TO TELL ME WHAT TO DO?

WHEN MOM TELLS ME IT'S TIME TO STOP DRAGGING THIS BLANKET AROUND THEN I'LL DO IT, BUT IT'S NO ONE ELSE'S BUSINESS, DO YOU HEAR ?!

HOORAY!

OH, SHUT UP!

ARE YOU ALL RIGHT, OL' BUDDY?

SOMETIMES I WAKE UP KNOWING I'M GOING TO HAVE A BAD DAY, AND, SURE ENOUGH, I HAVE A BAD DAY..

SOMETIMES I WAKE UP THINKING I'M GOING TO HAVE A GOOD DAY, BUT IT ALWAYS TURNS OUT TO BE A BAD DAY..

HOW COME I NEVER WAKE UP THINKING I'M GOING TO HAVE A GOOD DAY, AND THEN REALLY HAVE A GOOD DAY? OR HOW COME I NEVER WAKE UP THINKING I'M GOING TO HAVE A BAD DAY, AND THEN HAVE A GOOD DAY?

MY STOMACH HURTS..

I'M THINKING OF STARTING SOME NEW HOBBIES..

THAT'S A GOOD IDEA, LUCY.. THE PEOPLE WHO GET MOST OUT OF LIFE ARE THOSE WHO REALLY TRY TO ACCOMPLISH SOMETHING...

ACCOMPLISH SOMETHING?!

I THOUGHT WE WERE JUST SUPPOSED TO KEEP BUSY!

HERE'S A LIST OF SOME PLANTS WHICH ARE DANGEROUS FOR YOU TO EAT, SNOOPY...

ELEPHANT EAR, NARCISSUS, OLEANDER, BURNING BUSH, JIMSON WEED, MOUNTAIN LAUREL, LILY OF THE VALLEY, RHODODENDRON, SPIDER LILY AND FOXGLOVE...

THAT'S A SHAME..

I HAD MY STOMACH ALL SET FOR A LITTLE FOXGLOVE.

MY DAD HAS A DENTAL APPOINTMENT TODAY

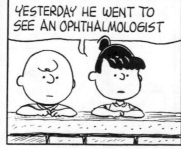
YESTERDAY HE WENT TO SEE AN OPHTHALMOLOGIST

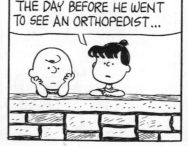
THE DAY BEFORE HE WENT TO SEE AN ORTHOPEDIST...

HE CONSIDERS IT ALL PART OF HIS COMPLETE PHYSICAL BREAKDOWN SINCE TURNING FORT...

HOW'S YOUR ARM THESE DAYS, CHARLIE BROWN?

IT FEELS FINE, THANK YOU..

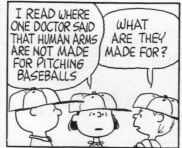
I READ WHERE ONE DOCTOR SAID THAT HUMAN ARMS ARE NOT MADE FOR PITCHING BASEBALLS

WHAT ARE THEY MADE FOR?

HUGGING!

HERE ARE SOME MORE PLANTS THAT ARE DANGEROUS FOR DOGS TO EAT, SNOOPY...

IVY LEAVES, DUMB CANE, MOCK ORANGE, CASTOR BEANS, FOUR O'CLOCK AND CYCLAMEN...

ALSO PIMPERNEL, SWEET PEA STEMS, BAYONET ROOTS, TULIP BULBS AND MONKSHOOD ROOTS

IT'S BEEN A LONG TIME SINCE THE GANG AND I USED TO SIT AROUND EATING MONKSHOOD ROOTS

I WONDER IF I'LL BE BEAUTIFUL WHEN I'M A SENIOR IN HIGH SCHOOL..

IF I KNEW I WASN'T GOING TO BE BEAUTIFUL, I WOULDN'T BOTHER HAVING GRADUATION PICTURES TAKEN...

CHUCK, WOULD YOU WANT MY GRADUATION PICTURE SITTING ON YOUR PIANO?

WE DON'T HAVE A PIANO

THAT'S WHAT I LIKE ABOUT YOU, CHUCK..YOU'RE ALWAYS RIGHT THERE WITH A QUICK WISHY-WASHY ANSWER!

It was a dark and stormy night.

MY NEW NOVEL IS GOING BADLY...

It was a dark and stormy night.

YOUR NEW NOVEL HAS A VERY EXCITING BEGINNING..

THANK YOU

GOOD LUCK WITH THE SECOND SENTENCE!

It was a dark and stormy night.

I HEAR YOU'RE WORKING ON A NEW NOVEL

I'M A GOOD ARTIST, SO IF YOU'LL START THINKING ABOUT WHAT YOU'D LIKE ON THE COVER OF YOUR BOOK, I'LL DRAW IT FOR YOU..

HOW ABOUT A BUNCH OF PIRATES AND FOREIGN LEGIONNAIRES FIGHTING SOME COWBOYS WITH SOME LIONS AND TIGERS AND ELEPHANTS LEAPING THROUGH THE AIR AT THIS GIRL WHO IS TIED TO A SUBMARINE?

It was a
dark and
stormy night.

Suddenly a shot rang out!

MY PLOT IS
THICKENING!

I'VE FINISHED
THE DRAWING FOR
THE COVER OF YOUR
NEW NOVEL...

SEE? IT SHOWS A BUNCH OF
PIRATES AND FOREIGN LEGIONNAIRES
FIGHTING SOME COWBOYS, AND SOME
LIONS AND TIGERS AND ELEPHANTS
LEAPING THROUGH THE AIR TOWARD A
GIRL WHO IS TIED TO A SUBMARINE

DID HE LIKE YOUR DRAWING?

IT NEEDS MORE TIGERS!

It was a dark
and stormy night.
Suddenly, a shot
rang out!

The maid screamed.
A door slammed.

Suddenly, a pirate ship
appeared on the horizon!

THIS TWIST IN THE PLOT
WILL BAFFLE MY READERS...

As he touched
her hand, she
sighed...

STOP RAINING
ON MY NOVEL!

And they lived
happily ever
after.

The End

FOR THE FIRST TIME IN
MY LIFE, I KNOW HOW
LEO MUST HAVE FELT...

LEO TOLSTOY, THAT IS!

RATS!

THEY NEVER HAVE ANY PROGRAMS THAT I LIKE..

I WONDER WHY NO ONE PUTS OUT WHAT I WOULD CONSIDER A PERFECT PROGRAM...

A FOUR-HOUR DOCUMENTARY ON BEAGLES!

GOOD GRIEF, MY CENTER-FIELDER IS FACING THE WRONG WAY!

HEY, THE BALL GAME IS **THIS** WAY!

I CAN'T FACE THAT WAY.. THE SUN SHINES IN MY EYES..I HAVE VERY SENSITIVE AND BEAUTIFUL EYES...

MAYBE YOU'D LIKE TO HAVE US MOVE THE WHOLE BALL FIELD AROUND IN FRONT OF YOU?

THAT'S A GOOD IDEA, CHARLIE BROWN...YOU DO THAT...I'LL STAY RIGHT HERE

I CAN'T STAND IT...I JUST CAN'T STAND IT!

I WONDER WHAT HE'S GOING TO PITCH TO THIS NEXT HITTER..

PROBABLY A CURVE BALL!

PSST, CHARLIE BROWN.....WE OUTFIELDERS HAVE BEEN WONDERING WHAT YOU'RE GOING TO PITCH TO THIS GUY..

A CURVE BALL

REALLY?

YOU WERE RIGHT! HE'S GONNA THROW HIM THE CURVE BALL!

ONE HUNDRED AND TWENTY-THREE TO NOTHING!

NO ONE SHOULD EVER HAVE TO LOSE THE FIRST GAME OF THE SEASON BY A SCORE OF 123 TO 0!

IT'S JUST NOT RIGHT..

BESIDES, HOW COULD WE POSSIBLY LOSE A GAME 123 TO 0?

WE NEVER GOT ANY BREAKS!

BEEP!

I HAVEN'T BEEPED YOU IN A LONG TIME

I HAVEN'T MISSED IT A BIT!

WHAT'S THIS?

"PROPOSED NEW DOG-FEEDING SCHEDULE"

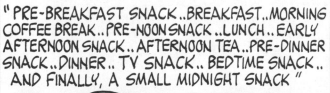

"PRE-BREAKFAST SNACK..BREAKFAST..MORNING COFFEE BREAK..PRE-NOON SNACK..LUNCH..EARLY AFTERNOON SNACK..AFTERNOON TEA..PRE-DINNER SNACK..DINNER..TV SNACK..BEDTIME SNACK.. AND FINALLY, A SMALL MIDNIGHT SNACK"

HMM...WELL, I'LL TELL YOU WHAT WE'LL DO... WE'LL COMPROMISE...

YOU'LL EAT ONE MEAL A DAY LIKE EVERY OTHER DOG!!!!

I HATE THOSE COMPROMISES!

SCHULZ

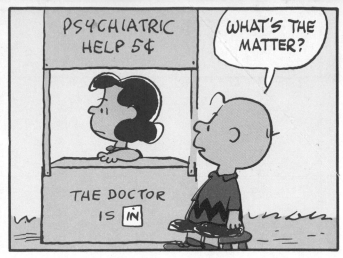

IS THIS YOUR BAT, CHARLIE BROWN? IT DOESN'T HAVE YOUR NAME ON IT...

YOU SHOULD HAVE YOUR NAME ON YOURS LIKE ALL OF THE BIG LEAGUE PLAYERS

LINUS HAS A WOOD-BURNING SET AT HOME... WHY DON'T I TAKE YOUR BAT, AND PUT YOUR NAME ON IT?

SAY! THIS IS GOING TO BE GREAT!

I'LL BE THE ONLY ONE AROUND HERE WITH HIS NAME ON A BAT!

THIS WILL REALLY IMPRESS THE KIDS ON THE OTHER TEAMS WE PLAY...THEY'LL BE AFRAID TO SEE ME STEP UP TO THE PLATE...THEY'LL THINK I'M A BIG-LEAGUER, AND I'LL...

HERE'S YOUR BAT, CHARLIE BROWN!

I HAD A LITTLE TROUBLE WITH THE WOOD-BURNING SET...

WELL, I GUESS I'M THE NEXT HITTER...

KEEP THE TRADEMARK UP, LUCY, AND THERE'LL BE LESS CHANCE OF CRACKING THE BAT..

OKAY, MANAGER.. ANYTHING YOU SAY!

STRIKE ONE!

STRIKE TWO!

STRIKE THREE!

YOU WERE RIGHT, MANAGER.. I KEPT THE TRADEMARK UP, AND I DIDN'T CRACK THE BAT!

MY STOMACH HURTS..

THIS GUY SAYS FOR ME TO TELL YOU THAT IF YOU THROW ANYTHING THAT EVEN **LOOKS** LIKE IT MIGHT BE A BEAN-BALL, HE'S GOING TO COME OUT HERE AND POUND YOU RIGHT INTO THE GROUND!

Z

BONK

WELL! DID THAT NASTY OL' POP FLY AWAKEN YOU? DID IT DISTURB YOUR BEAUTY SLEEP?

I'M SORRY IF THE SOUND OF FLY BALLS LANDING BEHIND YOU IS DEPRIVING YOU OF YOUR REST!

PERHAPS WE SHOULD SOFTEN THE INFIELD SO THE BALL WON'T MAKE SO MUCH NOISE WHEN IT LANDS BEHIND YOU...

WAAH!

OH, GOOD GRIEF! NOW, I'VE HURT HIS FEELINGS...

I'M SORRY, SNOOPY.. I APOLOGIZE..I SHOULDN'T HAVE BEEN SO SARCASTIC.. I GUESS I DON'T KNOW HOW TO HANDLE PLAYERS...I'M A TERRIBLE MANAGER... I APOLOGIZE..

SNIF

Z

BONK

ME?

SNOOPY?

REALLY?

SNOOPY HAS BEEN CHOSEN "ROOKIE OF THE YEAR"!

LOOK AT THE TROPHY THEY GAVE HIM!

AND THE BRONZE PLAQUE!

CONGRATULATIONS, SNOOPY; YOU DESERVED IT!

WOW! ONE OF MY OWN PLAYERS..ROOKIE OF THE YEAR! ISN'T THAT SOMETHING?

OKAY, TEAM! THAT PROVES WE'RE NOT SO BAD AFTER ALL! LET'S GET OUT THERE NOW AND WIN THIS GAME...LET'S SHOW 'EM HOW TO PLAY!

BONK!

I KNOW WHAT AWARD I'LL WIN.."STOMACH-ACHE OF THE YEAR"!

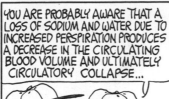

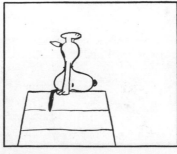

  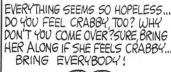   

HERE'S THE WORLD WAR I PILOT DOWN BEHIND ENEMY LINES...

IF I'M CAPTURED, I'LL BE SHOT AT DAWN...

I'LL SNEAK BACK INTO MY DAMAGED SOPWITH CAMEL, AND PUT ON MY SPECIAL DISGUISE..

WO IST DER ROOT BEER HALL?

HERE'S THE WORLD WAR I PILOT SITTING IN LITTLE RESTAURANT BEHIND ENEMY LINES

NO ONE RECOGNIZES ME IN MY VERY CLEVER DISGUISE

WHO'S THAT AT THE NEXT TABLE? HE LOOKS FAMILIAR.... GOOD GRIEF, IT'S THE RED BARON!

HI, RED!

AH, RED BARON, AT LAST WE MEET FACE TO FACE!

THERE IS RESPECT IN YOUR EYES, NO? YES, I AM THE FAMOUS PILOT WITH THE ALLIES

PERHAPS THERE IS ALSO A LITTLE FEAR IN YOUR EYES, NO?

NO!

PRISON! THEY THREW ME IN PRISON!

WHY DID I HAVE TO GIVE MYSELF AWAY IN THAT RESTAURANT? WHY DID I GO OVER AND TALK TO THE RED BARON?

NOW, I'LL SPEND THE REST OF WORLD WAR I IN THIS PRISON...THEY'LL NEVER LET ME OUT! NEVER!

OWOOOOOOOO

HERE'S THE WORLD WAR I FLYING ACE IN PRISON..

A GUARD!

I LEAP ON THE GUARD, AND WRESTLE HIM TO THE GROUND! JUDO CHOP! WHAM! WHAM! WHAM!

I'M FREE! I'M FREE! I'M FREE!

NEVER STICK YOUR HEAD INTO AN EMPTY DOG HOUSE!

OKAY, YOU STUPID BEAGLE...IT'S SUPPERTIME!

SUPPERTIME?

OH, IT'S SUPPERTIME! SUPPERTIME, SUPPERTIME, SUPPERTIME!

YES, IT'S SUPPERTIME, THE VERY BEST TIME OF DAY!! OH, IT'S SUPPERTIME! IT'S SUPPERTIME!

I FEEL LIKE I'M FEEDING FRED ASTAIRE!

DEAR SNOOPY, I AM WRITING FROM OUR MOTEL. WE ARE HAVING A NICE VACATION, BUT I MISS YOU.

SALLY SAYS, "HELLO"

I DIDN'T SAY "HELLO"

THIS IS TRADITIONAL VACATION POST CARD WRITING..YOU ALWAYS WRITE THAT SOMEONE SAYS, "HELLO"...YOU JUST DON'T UNDERSTAND VACATION POST CARD WRITING...

I DON'T EVEN UNDERSTAND VACATIONS!

HERE, YOU GOT A POST CARD..

PROBABLY A MESSAGE FROM CAPTAIN EDDIE RICKENBACKER

"RICK" WILL NEVER AMOUNT TO MUCH.. THOSE RACING DRIVERS DON'T KNOW ANYTHING ABOUT FLYING AIRPLANES

IT'S FROM YOUR MASTER WHO'S ON VACATION

MAYBE PRESIDENT WILSON IS WRITING AGAIN..HOW CAN I WIN THIS WAR IF HE KEEPS BOTHERING ME WITH ALL THESE POST CARDS?

DO YOU WANT ME TO READ IT TO YOU?

CAN YOU DECIPHER CODE, SWEETIE?

HOME AT LAST!

I'VE GOT TO GO GET SNOOPY! IF THAT LUCY WAS MEAN TO HIM, I'LL NEVER FORGIVE MYSELF

I NEVER SHOULD HAVE LEFT HIM WITH HER..WHY DID I DO IT? WHY?

IF THAT'S GENERAL PERSHING, TELL HIM I'M BUSY!

WELL, HOW WAS YOUR VACATION, CHARLIE BROWN?

VACATIONS ARE DREADED, SUFFERED, ENDURED, TOLERATED, SPOILED, RUINED AND WASTED...

VACATIONS CAN BE GREAT, TERRIBLE, WONDERFUL, AWFUL, DELIGHTFUL AND STUPID

I SPENT MY WHOLE VACATION WORRYING ABOUT MY DOG..

YOU NEED A VACATION, CHARLIE BROWN!

 HEY, SHORTSTOP! COME HERE A MINUTE, WILL YOU?

HOW ABOUT PLAYING JUST A LITTLE MORE TO YOUR RIGHT? OKAY, BABY? THAT'S THE BOY!

 THAT'S THE STRANGEST LITTLE KID I'VE EVER SEEN... HE NEVER SAYS ANYTHING!

 OKAY, TEAM, LET'S GET THIS NEXT GUY!

 WE CAN DO IT! WE CAN GET HIM EASY! HE'S NO HITTER! HE'S NO HITTER AT ALL!

  C'MON, TEAM, LET'S BEAR DOWN OUT THERE! LET'S REALLY GET THIS GUY!

 THAT'S THE ONLY PITCHER I'VE EVER KNOWN WHO SUPPLIED HER OWN INFIELD CHATTER!

 THIS IS RIDICULOUS!

  I'VE HIT FIVE HOME RUNS AND PITCHED A NO-HIT GAME, AND WE'RE BEHIND THIRTY-SEVEN TO FIVE! WHOEVER HEARD OF THIRTY-SEVEN UNEARNED RUNS? THIS IS RIDICULOUS!

 I THOUGHT I COULD HELP YOUR TEAM, CHUCK, BUT IT'S HOPELESS! I'M GOING BACK WHERE I CAME FROM!

THAT MUST BE A NICE THING TO BE ABLE TO DO...

 YOU'RE LEAVING? OF COURSE, I'M LEAVING! I CAN'T HELP THIS STUPID TEAM!

 SO LONG, MAC! YOU'RE THE ONLY DECENT PLAYER THEY'VE GOT!

HE'S A GOOD PLAYER, BUT I STILL THINK HE'S THE FUNNIEST LOOKING KID I'VE EVER SEEN!

 DEAR PEPPERMINT PATTY, I HOPE YOU HAD A NICE WALK HOME.

 I JUST WANTED YOU TO KNOW THAT I APPRECIATED YOUR COMING CLEAR ACROSS TOWN TO HELP OUR TEAM. SINCERELY,

"CHUCK"

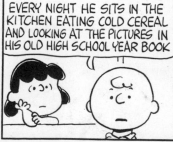

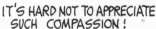

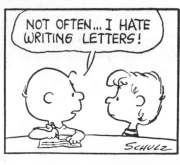

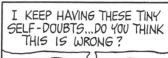

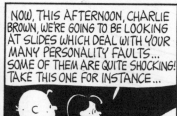

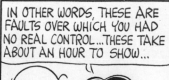

MY DAD IS KIND OF A PHILOSOPHER..

HE SAYS THAT THE GAME OF GOLF AND THE GAME OF LIFE ARE VERY SIMILAR...

THAT'S TRUE

UNFORTUNATELY, IN THE GAME OF LIFE, I'M ALWAYS HITTING FROM THE BACK TEES!

WHAT AM I, A "NEW FEMINIST," DOING STANDING OUT HERE IN CENTER FIELD?

THIS IS A MALE-DOMINATED GAME... WHY SHOULD I TAKE ORDERS FROM THAT STUPID MANAGER? I'M JUST AS GOOD AS HE IS! WHY SHOULD I STAND OUT HERE IN CENTER FIELD? THIS IS DEGRADING, AND I RESENT IT!

WHAP!!

NOW WHAT WAS THAT ALL ABOUT?

WHERE ARE ALL THE GIRLS WHO PLAY OUTFIELD?

THEY SAID THEY'RE NEW FEMINISTS, AND THEY REFUSE TO PLAY BASEBALL ANY MORE... I DON'T EVEN KNOW WHAT A NEW FEMINIST IS...

THE WORLD IS CHANGING, CHARLIE BROWN...

WHAT DOES THAT MEAN?

NO MATTER WHAT HAPPENS, I ALWAYS FEEL LIKE I'M IN THE NINTH INNING!

WE "NEW FEMINISTS" ARE GOING TO CHANGE THE WORLD!

WILL YOU STILL SMILE AND SAY, "GOOD MORNING"?

OF COURSE!

IF SOMEONE IS GOING AWAY AND IT'S RAINING, WILL YOU STILL GIVE HIM A HUG AND KISS HIM GOODBY?

OF COURSE!

BUT YOU STILL DON'T WANT TO PLAY CENTER FIELD?

NOPE! THAT'S DEGRADING!

✳ SIGH ✳

WELL, IT WAS ANOTHER BAD BASEBALL YEAR FOR ME..

MAYBE MY HERO, JOE SHLABOTNIK, IS HAVING A BETTER TIME... I'LL SEE HOW HE'S DOING...

"JOE SHLABOTNIK STRUCK OUT LAST NIGHT IN THE BOTTOM OF THE NINTH AS STUMPTOWN OF THE GREEN GRASS LEAGUE SANK DEEPER INTO THE CELLAR."

DEAR JOE, DON'T BE DISCOURAGE SOMEONE UNDERSTANDS

It

It was

It was a dark

It was a dark and stormy night.

GOOD WRITING IS HARD WORK!

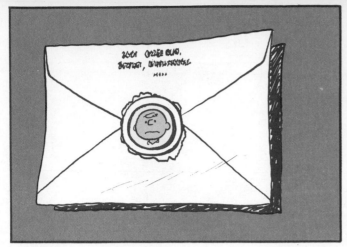

HERE'S THE WORLD WAR I FLYING ACE GOING INTO A LITTLE FRENCH CAFE NEAR APREMONT...

GARÇON! A ROOT BEER, PLEASE! WHY IS IT SO QUIET IN HERE? LET'S HAVE A LITTLE MUSIC!

WOULD MADEMOISELLE CARE TO DANCE? AH, SHE CANNOT RESIST THE CHARMS OF THE HANDSOME PILOT OF THE ALLIES...

"IT'S A LONG WAY TO TIPPERARY..."

GARÇON! MORE ROOT BEER! ROOT BEER FOR EVERYONE! WHEEEEE!!

VIVE LA FRANCE! VIVENT LES AMERICAINS!

CURSE THIS STUPID WAR!

WELL, LADS, THAT'S ENOUGH FOR TONIGHT... WE MUSTN'T FORGET THAT WE HAVE A JOB OF WORK TO DO!

THE SUN IS JUST COMING UP AS I REACH THE AERODROME..

HERE'S THE WORLD WAR I FLYING ACE TAKING OFF WITH THE DAWN PATROL...

SUDDENLY A RED FOKKER TRIPLANE APPEARS IN THE SKY!!

THE RED BARON IS SMART.. HE NEVER SPENDS THE WHOLE NIGHT DANCING AND DRINKING ROOT BEER..

GOOD NIGHT

HERE'S THE WORLD WAR I PILOT LYING IN A BED AT THE BASE HOSPITAL..

Z

THE MEMORY OF THE TERRIBLE DAYS IN THE SKY DRIVES SLEEP FROM HIS MIND...HIS NERVES ARE RAW...THE SOUND OF EXPLODING ANTI-AIRCRAFT FIRE DRUMS THROUGH HIS HEAD....

A FOKKER TRI-PLANE CUTS ACROSS HIS TAIL! MACHINE-GUN BULLETS SPLATTER THE SIDE OF HIS SOPWITH CAMEL! FLAMES! EXPLOSIONS! TERROR! OH, THE MEMORIES! THE FEAR!

SUDDENLY HE EMITS A TERRIBLE CRY OF ANGUISH....

AAUGHHH!

HERE'S THE WORLD WAR I PILOT BEING RETURNED TO HIS OUTFIT..

SCHULZ

DO YOU THINK THIS STATIONERY IS GOOD ENOUGH?

I'D HATE TO INSULT HIM BY USING CHEAP STATIONERY...

DEAR GREAT PUMPKIN, OH, HOW I LOOK FORWARD TO YOUR ARRIVAL ON HALLOWEEN NIGHT.

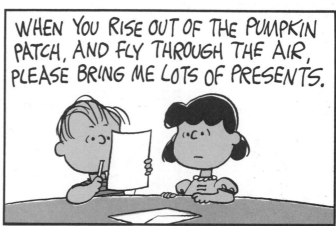

WHEN YOU RISE OUT OF THE PUMPKIN PATCH, AND FLY THROUGH THE AIR, PLEASE BRING ME LOTS OF PRESENTS.

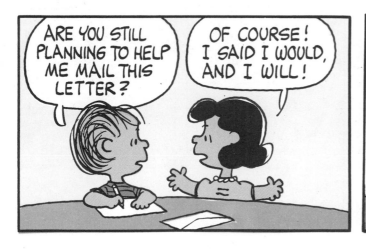

ARE YOU STILL PLANNING TO HELP ME MAIL THIS LETTER?

OF COURSE! I SAID I WOULD, AND I WILL!

MY SISTER LUCY IS GOING TO HELP ME MAIL THIS LETTER SO PLEASE BRING HER LOTS OF PRESENTS TOO.

HOW'S THAT?

FINE

GREED MAKES PEOPLE DO STRANGE THINGS..

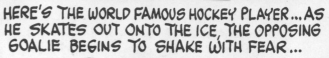

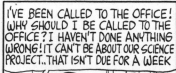

YOU LOOK WORRIED...

I AM WORRIED! WE'RE HAVING A TEST IN SCHOOL TOMORROW, AND THERE'S NO WAY I CAN PASS IT... ABSOLUTELY NO WAY!

HAVE YOU TRIED STUDYING?

WE'RE HAVING A TEST IN SCHOOL TOMORROW, AND THERE'S NO WAY I CAN PASS IT... ABSOLUTELY NO WAY!

WELL, ARE YOU ALL SET FOR THE 'TRUE OR FALSE' TEST TODAY?

TRUE OR FALSE? IS IT TRUE OR FALSE?!

WHEW! WHAT A RELIEF! I THOUGHT IT WOULD BE AN ESSAY TEST OR SOMETHING! WHEW! I'M SAVED!

TAKING A 'TRUE OR FALSE' TEST IS LIKE HAVING THE WIND AT YOUR BACK!

LET'S SEE NOW... IN A TRUE OR FALSE TEST, THE FIRST QUESTION IS ALMOST ALWAYS 'TRUE'...

THAT MEANS THE NEXT ONE WILL BE FALSE TO SORT OF BALANCE THE TRUE ONE.. THE NEXT ONE WILL ALSO BE FALSE TO BREAK THE PATTERN..

THEN ANOTHER TRUE AND THEN TWO MORE FALSE ONES AND THEN THREE TRUES IN A ROW...THEY ALWAYS HAVE THREE TRUES IN A ROW SOME PLACE...THEN ANOTHER FALSE AND ANOTHER TRUE...

IF YOU'RE SMART, YOU CAN PASS A TRUE OR FALSE TEST WITHOUT BEING SMART!

HOW DID YOU DO ON YOUR TEST?

DON'T ASK ME...IT WAS A DISASTER..

COULDN'T YOU EVEN PASS A TRUE OR FALSE TEST? WHAT HAPPENED?

I FALSED WHEN I SHOULD HAVE TRUED!

WELL, I HOPE YOU LEARNED A LESSON

YOU FAILED THAT TRUE OR FALSE TEST BECAUSE YOU DIDN'T STUDY

NO, I THINK I MERELY MISCALCULATED...

IF I HAD STARTED WITH A FALSE INSTEAD OF A TRUE, THEN THE THREE TRUES WOULD HAVE BEEN FALSES, AND THE FALSE THAT FOLLOWED THE TRUE WOULD HAVE...

OH, GOOD GRIEF!

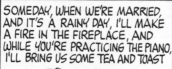

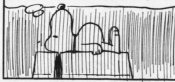

SCHOOL PRESIDENT? ME?

WHY NOT? I'LL BE YOUR CAMPAIGN MANAGER

BUT I COULD NEVER BE SCHOOL PRESIDENT.. THINK OF THE WORK.. THINK OF THE RESPONSIBILITY..

THINK OF THE POWER

I'LL DO IT!!

HERE...SIGN YOUR NAME ON THIS LINE..

WHEN WE GET TO SCHOOL, I'LL TAKE THIS INTO THE PRINCIPAL'S OFFICE, AND YOU WILL THEN BE OFFICIALLY ENTERED IN THE RACE FOR SCHOOL PRESIDENT!

GOOD...WE'RE ON OUR WAY!

I HOPE I WON'T BE EXPECTED TO DO SOMETHING RIGHT AWAY ABOUT TEACHERS' SALARIES...

I ACCEPT THE NOMINATION FOR THE OFFICE OF SCHOOL PRESIDENT..

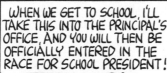
IF I AM ELECTED, I WILL DO AWAY WITH CAP AND GOWN KINDERGARTEN GRADUATIONS AND SIXTH GRADE DANCE PARTIES

IN MY ADMINISTRATION CHILDREN WILL BE CHILDREN AND ADULTS WILL BE ADULTS!!

I MAY EVEN DO AWAY WITH STUPID ELECTIONS LIKE THIS....THANK YOU..

I'VE DECIDED I WANT CHARLIE BROWN FOR MY VICE-PRESIDENT

OH, GOOD GRIEF!

WELL, WHAT'S **WRONG** WITH HIM? I THINK HE'D MAKE A **GOOD** VICE-PRESIDENT

MAYBE YOU'RE RIGHT..HE MIGHT EVEN HELP US WIN THE ELECTION

HE'LL PROBABLY BRING IN THE WISHY-WASHY VOTE!

I'VE BEEN TAKING A PRIVATE POLL OF THE VOTERS

I DON'T BELIEVE IN POLLS

THE WAY I SEE IT, YOU HAVE THE BACKLASH VOTE, THE FRONTLASH VOTE, THE WHIPLASH VOTE, THE EYELASH VOTE AND THE TONGUE LASH VOTE...

THIS WOULD GIVE YOU 73% AND YOUR OPPONENTS 22% WITH ONLY 5% UNDECIDED...

I BELIEVE IN POLLS!

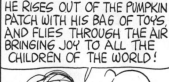

WE HAVE TO WRITE A BOOK REPORT ON "PETER RABBIT" FOR SCHOOL..

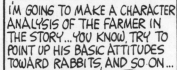

I'M GOING TO MAKE A CHARACTER ANALYSIS OF THE FARMER IN THE STORY...YOU KNOW, TRY TO POINT UP HIS BASIC ATTITUDES TOWARD RABBITS, AND SO ON...

I MAY EVEN BRING IN SOME SPECULATIONS ON HIS HOME LIFE WHICH COULD PROVE TO BE QUITE INTERESTING...

ALL IN ALL I HOPE TO UNCOVER SOME NEW TRUTHS ABOUT OUR CULTURE..

I THINK YOU ALREADY HAVE!

ANYONE WHO WOULD SIT AROUND BY HIMSELF MAKING FUNNY FACES MUST BE CRAZY

WHAT ELSE IS THERE TO DO ON A SATURDAY AFTERNOON WHEN YOUR GIRL FRIEND HAS LEFT YOU, YOUR TV SET IS BROKEN AND YOUR JOGGING SUIT IS IN THE WASH?

SEE THESE LEAVES, LINUS? THEY'RE FLYING SOUTH FOR THE WINTER!

WHAT MAKES YOU THINK THOSE LEAVES ARE FLYING SOUTH, LUCY?

WHEN YOU LOOK AT A MAP, NORTH IS UP AND SOUTH IS DOWN, ISN'T IT? WELL, ISN'T IT?

SEE THESE LEAVES, LINUS? THEY'RE FLYING SOUTH FOR THE WINTER!

NICE GOING...IT TOOK THAT STONE FOUR THOUSAND YEARS TO GET TO SHORE, AND NOW YOU'VE THROWN IT BACK!

EVERYTHING I DO MAKES ME FEEL GUILTY..

DEAR GREAT PUMPKIN, HALLOWEEN IS ALMOST HERE.

I'VE TOLD EVERYONE ABOUT YOUR COMING.

FORGIVE ME IF I SOUND BLUNT, BUT.......

IF YOU DON'T SHOW UP THIS YEAR, YOU'VE HAD IT!!

SNOOPY, I HAVE GREAT NEWS FOR YOU...

I AM GOING TO LET YOU SIT IN THE PUMPKIN PATCH WITH ME THIS YEAR, AND WAIT FOR THE ARRIVAL OF THE "GREAT PUMPKIN"!

HMM...TO QUOTE A WELL-WORN AND TIME-HONORED PHRASE...

"THRILLSVILLE!"

ON HALLOWEEN NIGHT THE "GREAT PUMPKIN" RISES OUT OF THE PUMPKIN PATCH THAT HE PICKS AS THE MOST SINCERE

THEN HE FLIES THROUGH THE AIR BRINGING TOYS TO ALL THE GOOD CHILDREN IN THE WORLD!

JUST THINK, SNOOPY, IF HE PICKS THIS PUMPKIN PATCH, YOU AND I WILL BE HERE TO SEE HIM!

FRANKLY, THIS LOOKS LIKE A GOOD PLACE TO GET MUGGED!

I WISH YOU COULD TALK, SNOOPY...

HERE YOU ARE SITTING IN A PUMPKIN PATCH WITH THE POSSIBILITY OF SEEING THE "GREAT PUMPKIN"... IT'S AN EMOTIONAL EXPERIENCE..

I'D REALLY BE INTERESTED IN KNOWING WHAT THOUGHTS ARE RUNNING THROUGH YOUR MIND...

WHEN DO WE EAT?

WHAT ARE YOU GUYS DOING?
WE'RE WAITING FOR THE "GREAT PUMPKIN"

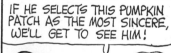
IF HE SELECTS THIS PUMPKIN PATCH AS THE MOST SINCERE, WE'LL GET TO SEE HIM!
OH, BROTHER..

I THINK YOU'RE BOTH CRAZY!
WE DON'T CARE WHAT YOU THINK, DO WE, SNOOPY?

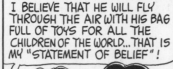

STUPID KID! I JUST HAD THAT CARPET IN THE FRONT HALL CLEANED!

RATS! I JUST CAN'T DO IT!!

WHAT'S THE MATTER, CHARLIE BROWN?

I CAN'T WRITE LIKE THE TEACHER WANTS US TO..

LOOK AT THIS BOOK...SEE HOW NICE ALL THE LETTERS ARE? I CAN'T WRITE LIKE THAT! I NEVER WILL BE ABLE TO WRITE LIKE THAT!

OF COURSE, YOU CAN'T, CHARLIE BROWN... NEITHER COULD THE PERSON WHO WROTE THIS BOOK.. WHAT HE DID, YOU SEE, WAS TAKE THE BEST LETTERS AND MAKE PHOTOSTATS OF THEM

THEN, FROM THESE PHOTOSTATS HE MADE A PASTE-UP OF THE WHOLE PAGE, AND PRINTED IT TO LOOK LIKE IT WAS DONE PERFECTLY..

YOU ARE A VICTIM OF STUDIO TECHNIQUE

WHOM DO I SUE?

HELLO, SCHROEDER? GUESS WHAT... I CALLED TO TELL YOU I'VE BEEN LISTENING TO SOME BEETHOVEN MUSIC

I'VE ALSO BEEN READING HIS BIOGRAPHY...IT'S VERY INTERESTING.. SORT OF SAD, AND YET SORT OF INSPIRING...YOU KNOW WHAT I MEAN?

I HAVE A POST CARD, TOO, THAT I THINK YOU'D LIKE...AN UNCLE OF MINE SENT IT TO ME FROM BONN, GERMANY...THEY HAVE A MUSEUM THERE

I GUESS THAT'S WHERE BEETHOVEN WAS BORN, ISN'T IT? I'LL BET YOU'D ENJOY VISITING THERE.. MAYBE YOU'LL HAVE A CHANCE TO SOMEDAY...

ANYWAY, THAT'S WHY I CALLED BECAUSE I KNEW YOU'D BE INTERESTED, AND I JUST WANTED TO TELL YOU ABOUT THESE THINGS...

IT'S NOT PROPER FOR A GIRL TO CALL A BOY ON THE TELEPHONE

AAUGH!!

HOW NICE OF HIM...HE JUST FLEW IN FROM GRENOBLE, AND HE SAID I WOULD HAVE WON EASILY!

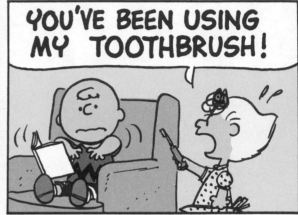

I'M DRAWING A ROW OF TREES, AND I'M GOING TO COLOR THEM GREEN

THAT'S NOT ART

I'LL PUT A LAKE IN FRONT OF THE TREES

THAT STILL WON'T MAKE IT ART

AND BY THE LAKE I'LL DRAW A TINY LOG CABIN

THAT'S NOT ENOUGH...YOU NEED A WATERFALL AND A SUNSET..SHOW THE SUN GOING DOWN SORT OF ORANGEY, AND PUT SOME RED STREAKS IN THE SKY, AND HAVE SOME SMOKE COMING OUT OF THE CHIMNEY

NOW PUT IN SOME MORE TREES...MAKE IT A FOREST... AND HAVE A DEER STANDING BY THE WATERFALL...THAT'S RIGHT...

NOW YOU HAVE TREES, A LAKE, A LOG CABIN, A WATERFALL, A DEER AND A SUNSET...

THAT'S ART!

SOMETIMES IT TAKES A LAYMAN TO SET THESE PEOPLE STRAIGHT

WHAT ARE *YOU* DOING HERE?

WHO WANTS TO KNOW? MAYBE I JUST LIKE MUSIC!

DO YOU LIKE BEETHOVEN?

WHAT?

IF YOU'RE GOING TO HANG AROUND HERE, YOU'VE GOT TO LIKE BEETHOVEN...

ALL RIGHT, BUT I'LL JUST HAVE A SMALL GLASS

KLUNK!

YOU BLEW IT, KID!

TOMORROW IS BEETHOVEN'S BIRTHDAY..

I HAVE AN IDEA FOR A GREAT PARTY!

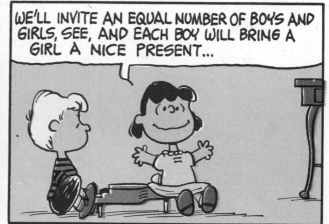

WE'LL INVITE AN EQUAL NUMBER OF BOYS AND GIRLS, SEE, AND EACH BOY WILL BRING A GIRL A NICE PRESENT...

AT THE APPOINTED TIME, EACH GIRL WILL OPEN HER PRESENT, AND THEN EACH GIRL WILL GIVE EACH BOY A WARM HUG AND A KISS!

TOMORROW IS BEETHOVEN'S BIRTHDAY..

I SHALL CELEBRATE HIS BIRTHDAY BY PLAYING HIS SONATA IN A FLAT MAJOR, OPUS 110, AND SITTING IN SILENT MEDITATION FOR ONE MINUTE... BY MYSELF!

TOMORROW IS MONDAY..

I CAN'T SLEEP!

MAYBE IF I MOVE AROUND AND TRY DIFFERENT POSITIONS...

RATS! I JUST CAN'T GET COMFORTABLE!

SNOOPY?

SNOOPY?

WHERE'D HE GO?

Z

OKAY, I'M READY... THROW ME THE HOCKEY BALL!

YOU INVITED HER.. I DIDN'T

I LOVE PLAYING HOCKEY BALL!

NOW HERE'S THE WAY WE START THE GAME..

WE HAVE A "FACE-OFF" SEE... WE LEAN OVER AND TAP OUR STICKS TOGETHER THREE TIMES.... OKAY, LET'S GO...

SMAK!

PENALTY BOX

NUMBERS ARE BEAUTIFUL..

I LIKE TWOS THE BEST...THEY'RE SORT OF GENTLE..THREES AND FIVES ARE MEAN, BUT A FOUR IS ALWAYS PLEASANT.. I LIKE SEVENS AND EIGHTS, TOO, BUT NINES ALWAYS SCARE ME...TENS ARE GREAT...

HAVE YOU DONE THOSE DIVISION PROBLEMS FOR TOMORROW?

NOTHING SPOILS NUMBERS FASTER THAN A LOT OF ARITHMETIC!

HAPPY BEETHOVEN'S BIRTHDAY!

SMACK!

ON BEETHOVEN'S BIRTHDAY IT HAS BECOME TRADITIONAL TO KISS EVERYONE ON THE NOSE

FORGET IT !!

HERE'S THE WORLD-FAMOUS HOCKEY PLAYER TAPING HIS STICK BEFORE THE GAME..

WE HOCKEY PLAYERS ARE VERY FUSSY ABOUT THE WAY WE TAPE OUR STICKS

SOMETIMES, OF COURSE, WE HAVE A LITTLE TROUBLE WITH THE TAPE...

IT'S RIDICULOUS FOR ME TO WRITE TO A PEN-PAL IN PENCIL!

I'M GOING TO LEARN TO WRITE WITH A PEN IF IT KILLS ME!

DEAR PEN-PAL, I HAVE TO WRITE

SORRY.... I GOT KIND OF CARRIED AWAY...

RATS!
I THINK YOU'RE TOO TENSE WHEN YOU TRY TO WRITE WITH A PEN, CHARLIE BROWN...

BEFORE YOU BEGIN, YOU SHOULD SORT OF SWIRL YOUR PEN AROUND A BIT TO LOOSEN UP

THAT'S THE WAY... MOVE YOUR WHOLE ARM AROUND... FASTER! 'ROUND AND AROUND...

THOSE WERE GOOD SWIRLS...

DEAR PEN PAL, TODAY I TAKE PEN IN HAND.

I AM VERY PROUD OF MYSELF.

SO FAR I HAVEN'T SMEARED A SINGLE

WORD

HERE'S THE WORLD FAMOUS HOCKEY PLAYER STANDING AT ATTENTION WHILE THEY PLAY THE NATIONAL ANTHEM

WHAT AN INSPIRING MOMENT!

BEAUTIFUL!

TEN MORE SECONDS, AND I CAN CLOBBER SOMEBODY!

I will not talk in class. I will not talk in class.

I will not talk in class. I will not talk in class. I will not talk in class.

I will not talk in class. I will not talk in class. I will not talk in class.

On the other hand, who knows what I'll do?

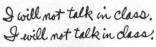

OUR TEACHER, MISS OTHMAR, STAYED HOME TODAY...

YESTERDAY, WE HAD TO BRING MILK MONEY ENVELOPES, CLASS PICTURE MONEY ENVELOPES, PTA MONEY ENVELOPES AND HOT DOG MONEY ENVELOPES...

THIRTY KIDS BRINGING FOUR ENVELOPES EACH MAKES ONE HUNDRED AND TWENTY ENVELOPES.. POOR MISS OTHMAR...

SHE CRACKED UP... SHE WENT "ENVELOPE HAPPY"!

MISS OTHMAR CAME BACK TO SCHOOL TODAY, BUT SHE DIDN'T LAST VERY LONG..

SEVEN KIDS HAD ABSENCE EXCUSES IN ENVELOPES...

TWENTY-EIGHT OTHERS BROUGHT BACK VACCINATION NOTICES WHICH THEIR PARENTS HAD SIGNED..... POOR MISS OTHMAR...

THAT'S THE FIRST TIME I'VE EVER SEEN A TEACHER CRAWL RIGHT UP THE CHALKBOARD!

DEAR MISS OTHMAR, I HOPE YOU ARE FEELING BETTER.

I DON'T BLAME YOU FOR GETTING UPSET THE OTHER DAY.

YOU WERE A SIGHT RUNNING DOWN THE HALL SCREAMING AND THROWING THOSE ENVELOPES ALL OVER.

REST QUIETLY. DON'T WORRY ABOUT US.
YOUR PUPIL,
LINUS

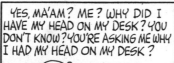

SO HERE I AM IN THE PRINCIPAL'S OFFICE...GOOD GRIEF!

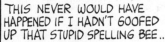
THIS NEVER WOULD HAVE HAPPENED IF I HADN'T GOOFED UP THAT STUPID SPELLING BEE..

WHEN THE TEACHER SAID FOR ME TO SPELL "MAZE," THE FIRST THING THAT CAME TO MY MIND WAS WILLIE MAYS....OH, WELL...

MAYBE SOMEDAY AFTER I'M GROWN UP, I'LL MEET WILLIE MAYS, AND I'LL TELL HIM WHAT HAPPENED, AND WE'LL HAVE A GOOD LAUGH TOGETHER

YES, SIR...I WAS TOLD BY MY TEACHER TO COME TO YOUR OFFICE...

NO, I'VE NEVER BEEN HERE BEFORE.. I'VE NEVER DONE ANYTHING REALLY WRONG BEFORE......

YOU HAVE A NICE OFFICE..

HOW ARE YOU AND THE P.T.A. GETTING ALONG?

NO, SIR, I DON'T THINK IT WAS RIGHT TO YELL AT MRS. DONOVAN, MY TEACHER..
WHAT DO I THINK MY FATHER WILL SAY?!

WELL, SIR, HE'S A VERY UNDERSTANDING PERSON...I REALLY THINK THAT WHEN I EXPLAIN THE WHOLE STORY, HE'LL UNDERSTAND...HE WON'T CONDEMN ME...

HE'S LEARNED A LOT ABOUT PEOPLE IN HIS BARBER SHOP, AND HE KNOWS HOW THINGS SOMETIMES JUST SORT OF HAPPEN...SO I DON'T THINK HE'LL SAY MUCH....MOM IS THE SAME WAY...

I DO HAVE A FEW FRIENDS, HOWEVER, WHO MIGHT HAVE SOME THOUGHTS ON THE SUBJECT!

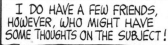

GOOD GRIEF! STANDING IN FRONT OF ALL THESE ADULTS' DESKS MAKES YOU FEEL LIKE YOU'RE IN A PIT!

MRS. DONOVAN, I WANT TO APOLOGIZE FOR YELLING AT YOU...IT WAS VERY RUDE OF ME, AND I'M SORRY...

OH, INCIDENTALLY.... M...A...Z...E!

BOY, WHAT A DAY...THIS HAS BEEN THE WORST DAY OF MY LIFE!

I WOKE UP THIS MORNING LOOKING FORWARD TO THE SPELLING BEE, AND I END UP IN THE PRINCIPAL'S OFFICE.... GOOD GRIEF!

ON A DAY LIKE THIS, A PERSON REALLY NEEDS HIS FAITHFUL DOG TO COME RUNNING OUT TO GREET HIM ...

HERE'S THE WORLD WAR I PILOT IN HIS FIGHTER PLANE LOOKING FOR THE RED BARON!
SIGH

DEAR AGNES, I LIKE YOUR ADVICE COLUMN IN THE PAPER.

I FEEL THAT I COULD USE SOME OF YOUR ADVICE MYSELF.

I DON'T KNOW, HOWEVER, EXACTLY WHAT IT IS THAT I WANT TO ASK YOU.

JUST SEND ME SOME ADVICE.

DID THE LITTLE BOY WHO SITS IN FRONT OF YOU AT SCHOOL CRY AGAIN TODAY?

HE CRIES EVERY DAY! HE HAS ALL THE SIMPLE CHILDHOOD FEARS... FEAR OF BEING LATE FOR SCHOOL, FEAR OF HIS TEACHER, AND FEAR OF THE PRINCIPAL...

FEAR OF NOT KNOWING WHAT ROOM TO GO TO AFTER RECESS, FEAR OF FORGETTING HIS LUNCH, FEAR OF BIGGER KIDS, FEAR OF BEING ASKED TO RECITE...

FEAR OF MISSING THE SCHOOL BUS, FEAR OF NOT KNOWING WHEN TO GET OFF THE SCHOOL BUS, FEAR OF...

GOOD GRIEF!

HELLO?

I WANT TO TALK ABOUT FOREIGN AFFAIRS AND WHAT'S HAPPENING OVERSEAS AND LITTLE KIDS AND HIGH PRICES AND OLD MOVIES...

AND I DON'T LIKE RECENT TRENDS AND WHAT THEY'RE ALL SAYING, AND I WANT TO PUT IN A GOOD WORD FOR THE TREES... OKAY... ...THANK YOU.... GOOD-BYE ....

I LIKE THESE PHONE-IN RADIO SHOWS!

HELLO? I'M ONE OF YOUR REGULAR CALLERS, YOU KNOW?

I ENJOY YOUR PROGRAM, AND, YOU KNOW, THE THINGS PEOPLE CALL IN ABOUT, YOU KNOW....

WELL, I JUST WANTED TO SORT OF, YOU KNOW, SAY THAT I THINK YOU'RE DOING A GOOD JOB, YOU KNOW...YOU'RE WELCOME.....AND, WELL, YOU KNOW...GOOD-BYE...

WE CALLERS TO PHONE-IN RADIO SHOWS SAY "YOU KNOW" QUITE A LOT!

HELLO? SAY, ABOUT THAT LAST CALLER YOU HAD ON THERE...

WHAT IS HE, SOME KIND OF FAR-OUT NUT, OR WHAT? IF HE DOESN'T LIKE THIS WORLD, WHY DOESN'T HE LEAVE?

I THINK I KNOW WHAT'S GOOD AND RIGHT AND WRONG OR I THINK WHO'S DOING WHAT THEY THINK IS THE TROUBLE WITH ALL THIS FOOLISHNESS, YOU KNOW, AND I'M SURE!! YOU'RE WELCOME..GOOD BYE..

THESE PHONE-IN RADIO SHOWS SURE HAVE SOME WEIRD CALLERS!

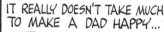

HERE'S THE WORLD FAMOUS FIGURE SKATER PRACTICING HIS "OUTSIDE EIGHTS"

HE REALIZES THAT HE MUST PRACTICE DILIGENTLY IF HE IS TO WIN A GOLD MEDAL AT THE OLYMPICS...

ACTUALLY, VERY FEW BEAGLES ARE EVER INVITED TO THE OLYMPICS!

HERE'S THE WORLD FAMOUS FIGURE SKATER PRACTICING FOR THE OLYMPICS IN GRENOBLE...

TODAY I'M WORKING ON MY "DOUBLE AXEL"

THEY'RE GOING TO LOVE ME IN GRENOBLE!

REAL FIGURE SKATERS SMILE A LOT...

MAYBE JUST A PLEASANT GRIN WOULD BE BETTER...

DID YOU KNOW THAT YOUR STUPID DOG THINKS HE'S GOING TO GRENOBLE TO SKATE IN THE OLYMPICS?

GRENOBLE IS IN FRANCE! HOW CAN HE GO TO GRENOBLE?

HOW CAN A STUPID BEAGLE EVER GO TO GRENOBLE?!

WE BEAGLES DO A LOT OF PECULIAR THINGS!

STUPID DOG!

GRENOBLE?

I HEAR YOU'RE PRACTICING FOR THE OLYMPICS...

DID YOU KNOW THEY'RE BEING HELD IN GRENOBLE, FRANCE?

DO YOU KNOW WHERE GRENOBLE IS?

I DON'T EVEN KNOW WHERE FRANCE IS!

CAR SALE!

YES, YOU HEARD RIGHT! YOU'VE NEVER SEEN SUCH VALUES!

COME DOWN TO OUR SHOWROOM NOW!!

DON'T DELAY!! COME DOWN **NOW**! NOW IS THE TIME! **NOW! NOW! NOW!**

HELP!

IF YOU HIT ME WITH THAT SNOWBALL, I'LL **CLOBBER** YOU WITH THIS ONE!

ARE YOU GOING TO LET HER BLUFF YOU THAT WAY?

NEVER TRADE A HIT FOR A CLOBBER!

YOU DISLIKE ME, DON'T YOU?

YOU HATE ME... YOU DETEST ME... YOU LOATHE ME... YOU ABHOR ME... YOU DESPISE ME..

I'VE NEVER SAID THAT I DESPISE YOU

REALLY?

LET'S WORK OUR WAY BACKWARD THROUGH THAT LIST...

LISTEN..

DON'T YOU THINK SOME NICE MUSIC IN THE MORNING IS A GOOD WAY TO START THE DAY?

I NEVER WORRY ABOUT HOW I START THE DAY...

IT'S HOW IT ENDS UP THAT BOTHERS ME!

HERE'S THE WORLD-FAMOUS HOCKEY GOALIE GUARDING THE NET..

AAUGH!

NOBODY SCORES!

DEAR SANTA CLAUS, JUST A LITTLE NOTE BEFORE YOU TAKE OFF.

I ALWAYS WORRY ABOUT YOU. I HOPE YOU ARE IN GOOD HEALTH. PLEASE DRIVE CAREFULLY.

HAVE A GOOD TRIP. AFFECTIONATELY YOURS, LUCY VAN PELT (YOUR FRIEND) P.S. MERRY CHRISTMAS LUCY (YOUR VERY GOOD FRIEND) X X X X X X X X ← KISSES

BLEAH!

MERRY CHRISTMAS, CHARLIE BROWN!

AT THIS TIME OF YEAR I THINK WE SHOULD PUT ASIDE ALL OUR DIFFERENCES, AND TRY TO BE KIND

WHY DOES IT HAVE TO BE FOR JUST THIS TIME OF YEAR? WHY CAN'T IT BE ALL YEAR 'ROUND?

WHAT ARE YOU, SOME KIND OF FANATIC OR SOMETHING?

WELL, LINUS, DID YOU HAVE A GOOD CHRISTMAS? WHAT DO YOU MEAN BY "GOOD"?

DO YOU MEAN DID I GET A LOT OF PRESENTS? OR DO YOU MEAN DID I GIVE A LOT OF PRESENTS?

ARE YOU REFERRING TO THE WEATHER OR THE CHRISTMAS DINNER WE HAD? DO YOU MEAN WAS MY CHRISTMAS GOOD IN A SPIRITUAL SENSE?

DO YOU MEAN WAS MY CHRISTMAS GOOD IN THAT I SAW NEW MEANING IN OLD THINGS? OR DO YOU MEAN... SIGH

FOR THREE MONTHS I COUNTED THE DAYS UNTIL CHRISTMAS..

THEN LAST WEEK I STARTED TO COUNT THE HOURS...

THEN ON CHRISTMAS EVE I STARTED TO COUNT THE MINUTES; THEN THE SECONDS... I COUNTED EVERY SECOND UNTIL CHRISTMAS...

AND NOW IT'S ALL OVER!

WELL, THIS IS IT..

THE LAST DAY OF THE YEAR, AND I DID IT AGAIN

DID WHAT?

I BLEW ANOTHER YEAR!